Beginner To Pro

Blackjack Made Easy

by
Stephen Mead

© Copyright Stephen Mead 2002

Mead Publishing Company, Inc.
3111 E. Texas #207 - Bossier City - LA 71111

ISBN   0-9718298-0-2
Printed in the United States of America
Library of Congress Catalog Number 2002090497

First Printing

Mead Publishing Company, Inc.
3111 E. Texas #207 - Bossier City - LA 71111

To my two wonderful children,
Samantha and Christopher, whom I
love with all my heart.

3

Acknowledgments.

I would like to thank my good friend Brian Williamson for his invaluable help and advice in correcting my uniquely flawed punctuation and grammar and for being a good friend in my hour of need.

Additionally I would like to express my gratitude to The Press of Atlantic City, New Jersey for the use of their article.

Contents.

Charts.

Introduction.

In the last few years many new casinos have opened their doors around the United States. This huge advance in the casino industry has introduced millions of Americans to an atmosphere they are unfamiliar with. Gambling. Some of these people may be comfortable in this environment, maybe they have been to Las Vegas or Atlantic City, but the larger percentage are novices looking for an easy way to increase their chances of winning. Of all the games in the casino, Blackjack is one of the few where the player has the ability to directly affect the outcome of their bet.

There have been many books written on the subject of Blackjack over the years but most are now old and out of date. "Playing Blackjack as a Business" by Lawrence Revere, (the original bible of Blackjack), and Edward Thorp's "Beat The Dealer", while both being significantly good books, were originally written in the 1960's. Since then many changes have been made in the casino industry.

Also many books tend to fill out their pages with information not needed, that is complex and in depth containing numerous confusing graphs and charts or packed full of facts, figures, percentages and other overwhelming information that even a rocket scientist would have trouble understanding. Most of this information you will never need. You don't have to know why you hit 16 against the dealer's 10. Nor do you need intricate charts telling you in great detail how many times out of a thousand you will win or lose with this or that hand. All that you need to know is that with 16 against a 10 you hit.

My aim is to show you, clearly, concisely, and in easy to understand terms that You Can Win!

I have worked behind the tables in the casino industry for over fifteen years in Europe, on Cruise Ships and in the United States, and have seen countless thousands of people lose their money, (in some cases huge fortunes), across the tables all because of one main reason. They didn't know how to play! Their play is erratic and inconsistent. Sometimes they will hit 15 against the dealer's 9 and sometimes they will stand. Sometimes they will double down on 11 and sometimes not. They will automatically split pairs, most times without ever looking to see the dealer's up-card. Money management is almost non-existent. They will play hunches and chase their losses, betting with money they cannot afford to lose. They will let superstition get the better of them, or worse still their temper. All of these are cardinal mistakes and any one of them will result in the eventual loss of their money yet, if you ask them they will tell you that "They know what

9

they are doing" or "Have been playing for years". They have been losing for years.

In this book I will teach you in the simplest way possible how to win. You will find no confusing or unnecessary facts and figures. Only the information you will need to become a winner. You do not need an extraordinarily high I.Q. in order to count cards or to learn proper basic strategy. All that you need is the time to practice and the willingness to learn.

Read carefully through this book learning one chapter at a time. Take your time with each section. Do not start reading the next chapter until you are completely confident with what you have just learned. Don't run before you can walk, and in just a few weeks you will have learned more about the game of Blackjack than most players will learn in a lifetime.

How The Game Is Played.

In Blackjack everybody plays against the dealer. It is played with one (1) to eight (8) decks of cards dealt from a shoe. All picture cards or "face cards", (Jack, Queen, King), count as ten. The Ace counts as 1 or 11, your choice. All other cards count as face value. The object of the game is to beat the dealer by getting as close to 21 as possible without going "over" or "bust".

First the players make their bets by placing "chips" or "tokens" in the box provided. The dealer will then give everyone two cards, face-up, and himself two cards, one face-up and the other face-down underneath the first. This is known as the dealers "hole" card. You will then be given the opportunity to improve your hand by either "Hitting", "Splitting", "Double Down" or if you would like to "Stand". These options are to your advantage as you can use them as you prefer whereas the dealer has to follow a strict set of given rules. I shall show you how to use this advantage to the full as we develop further into this book.

All winning bets are paid "even money", ($5 pays $5), with the exception of Blackjack which pays 3-2 or one and a half times the bet, ($5 pays $7.50). A draw or a tie is called a "push" or "stand-off" and remains in place.

Blackjack.

The name of the game. If your first two (2) cards equal 21, (an ace with any 10, jack, queen or king), it is a natural "Blackjack" and is paid 3-2. If both you and the dealer have Blackjack it is a push. If the dealer has an ace showing you have the option of taking "even-money", (see Insurance).

Note: A Blackjack, (2 cards), beats 21, (3 or more cards).

Hit or Stand.

After the dealer puts out the first two cards you have the option to take more cards in order to improve your hand. Taking a card is called a "Hit". You may take as many cards as you wish, letting the dealer know by tapping the table next to your cards. If you go over 21 you "bust" and automatically lose your bet. The dealer will immediately remove your money and your cards.

If you feel that your hand is good enough you may elect to "Stand". This is done by waving your hand from side to side over your cards. At no time should you touch the cards.

Soft Totals.

If your hand is made up of an Ace and any other card this is called a "soft" total. A hand where it is impossible to bust. An Ace counts as 1 or 11, whichever you prefer.   If you take a card that puts your soft total over 21 it immediately becomes a hard total.

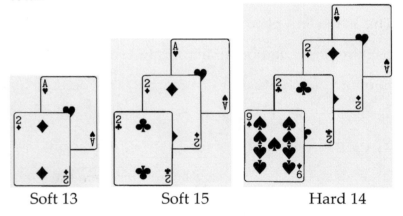

Soft 13   Soft 15   Hard 14

Double Down.

You may elect to "double down" your hand against the dealer. In short you are adding to your bet because you are confident you will win. The catch? You only get one more card, no matter what it may be. You make your double down bet by placing chips of the same amount next to your original bet.

This can only be done on the first two cards of your hand.

Some casinos will let you double down for less. This is never a good idea as you are taking all of the risk by only getting one card but only getting a portion of the rewards if you win.

Splitting Pairs.

If the first two cards of your hand are the same point total, (2-2, 8-8, etc), you may want to "split" your hand. This is done by putting the same amount of money next to your bet. No more, no less. It must be the exact same amount. The dealer will then split your cards into two separate hands. He will give a card to the first, making it a two card hand. You may then make a decision as to what you now wish to do, hit, stand, double down or split again. After you have finished with the first hand you immediately move to the next. From the point of the split they are treated as entirely separate hands.

If you get another card of the same original point total you may elect to split again. Each casino varies as to how many times they will let you split pairs. If you are unsure, just ask the dealer and they will be happy to help.

Splitting Aces.

When you split Aces, which you would always do, you only get one card for each Ace. You will not be allowed to hit the hand regardless of the point total. Some casinos will allow you split Aces more than once but these are sometimes hard to find.

Note: If you split Aces and get a 10 value card it counts only as 21, not Blackjack.

Insurance.

If the dealers up card is an Ace you may elect to take "insurance". This is done by placing up to half of your bet on the insurance line. It must be done before anyone takes a card. The dealer will then "peek" at his hole card. If the dealer does not have Blackjack the insurance bet loses and the hand carries on as normal.

If the dealer does have Blackjack the original bet loses but the insurance bet gets paid 2-1, protecting the original bet.

If you have a Blackjack against the dealers Ace you have the option of taking "even-money". If you decide upon taking it the dealer will pay you even-money on your flat bet and take your cards. This works out exactly the same as insurance.

Surrender.

If, after your first two cards, you think that you have no chance of winning you may want to "surrender" your bet. This must be done before you take a hit or make any decision on your hand. If taken the dealer will take half of your bet and your cards, returning the remaining portion of your money to you.

There are two types of surrender. Early Surrender, where you may surrender your hand straight away and against any hand, and Late Surrender, when the dealer will first check his hand for Blackjack. If he has Blackjack you still lose. These rules can vary greatly from casino to casino but most will offer the latter.

Note: Before taking Insurance you should realize that out of the thirteen different cards in the deck, four of them are tens, nine of them are not. It is more than 2-1 that the dealer does not have Blackjack. The casino will win on the Insurance bet 69% of the time. Out of hundred hands you will win two units on the insurance bet thirty-one times and the casino will win one unit sixty-nine times. They will be ahead by seven units. That's a juicy 7% edge! The casino wants you to think that Insurance will somehow save your Blackjack against a push, (even money), but don't be fooled. Insurance is a separate bet AGAINST your hand. It's a bad bet because the odds favor your Ace and ten. You will earn more money in the long run (69% of the time) skipping the insurance and taking the 3-2 payment.

Both Insurance and Surrender are heavily weighted in favor of the house and should never be taken, unless you are counting cards. They are known colloquially as "Sucker Bets".

The History Of Blackjack.

It is believed that playing cards were originally invented in China, home to one of the oldest cultures in the world, sometime around 900 A.D. The Chinese are thought to have originated card games when they began shuffling paper money, (another Chinese invention), into various combinations. Today in China, the general term for playing cards means "paper tickets". The 52 card deck as we know it today in the United States was originally referred to as the "French Pack" which was later adopted by the English and subsequently the Americans.

The first real accounts of gambling were in 2300 B.C. or so, and yes, the Chinese once again get the credit. Gambling was also a very popular pastime in Ancient Greece, even though it was illegal, and has been a part of the human experience ever since.

In the United States gambling was legal out West from the 1850's to 1910, at which time it became a felony to operate a gambling game in Nevada. In 1931 Nevada re-legalized casino gambling and Blackjack became one of the primary games of chance offered to gamblers.

In 1978 casino gambling was legalized in Atlantic City, New Jersey and as of 1989 only these two states had legalized casino gambling. Since then however, many states have legalized gambling in some form or another and casino's can now be found almost anywhere there is an Indian Reservation or large river.

The origins of the game of Blackjack have been heavily disputed between France and Italy for many years with both countries claiming it as their own. Also known as Vingt et Un or Twenty-One it is one of the world's most popular gambling games.

While the French claim there is a relationship to their French Ferme and Chemin de Fer the Italians allege a similarity to their Seven and a Half. Both of these games are definitely similar in structure to Blackjack. Since the late 1400's many versions of the game have existed in many countries. Shown here are a few examples of the most well known versions.

Pontoon, (England), also known as **Van John**, (Australia), is played in the same manner as Blackjack with just a few minor alterations plus the added attraction of bonus pay-outs. If a player makes 21 or less with five cards this is paid 2-1. With six cards 21 or less pays 4-1 and so on doubling the payout with each additional card. 21 made with three 7's pays 3-1 and if a player making 21 with a six, seven and eight, (a straight), will be paid 2-1. The dealer does not receive bonuses.

Fifteen or **Quince**, (France), is a game for two players. In this game, also known as **Ace-Low** or **Cans**, all basic Blackjack rules apply except now instead of 21 the target figure is now 15 without going over. Also the Ace counts as one (1) only.

Seven and a Half, (Italy), is a one deck game. In this version all 8's, 9's and 10's have been removed making up a 40 card deck including two jokers. Picture cards count as 1/2 while all other cards are face value. The joker may be used as any card. The object now is to make 7 1/2 or as close as possible without going over.

Ten and a Half, (Holland), is a Dutch version also referred to locally as **Satan Pong**. This game is played almost the same as Seven and a Half except all cards from the deck are used. Picture cards count as 1/2 and all others, including tens, are face value. The object now is 10 1/2.

Macao, also known as **Three Naturals**, was a popular game during the 1920's but today is not so common. Played as a cross between Blackjack and Baccarat the object is to obtain a total of 9 or less with one or more cards. Each player and the dealer receive one card, face down. A natural 7, 8 or 9 is paid instantly. 9 pays 3-1, 8 pays 2-1 and 7 gets even-money. Then the game continues with each player in turn drawing cards to achieve as close to 9 as possible without going over. If the dealer does not have a natural 7, 8 or 9 he/she then draws to 9 also.

Chemin de Fer, (France - Italy), is also known as **Baccarat, Baccarat-Chemin de Fer, Punto-Banco**, Baccarat **Banque** or **Shemmy**. The present day forms of Baccarat and Chemin de Fer are versions of the

Italian game of Baccara. First introduced into France in the 1490's during the reign of Charles VIII, this is possibly the source of the argument between France and Italy as to who originated the game of Blackjack.

Two versions of Blackjack widely exist. There is the private game played at home or among friends where every player has the option of being dealer or banker and the rules can vary greatly depending upon the preferences of the players, five card charlie's etc. Then there is the professional game played in casinos around the world where a dealer is provided and the house retains the bank. Here the rules are rigid with controlling bodies such as gaming boards, usually run by the state or government, overseeing.

Basic Strategy.

Of all the casino games Blackjack is one of the very few where you, the player, can have the ability to directly affect the outcome of your wager. There are many ways in which you could play a hand. Hunches, gut instinct or superstition could have a hand in all, but the smart player employs just one method. Mathematical probability.

To consistently win in Blackjack is not just luck, it's mathematical. An intelligent gambler will strictly adhere to a proven set of decision rules that have been developed through computer analysis that provides the best possible decision for each hand played. There are many people who do not believe in "Basic Strategy" because they once took the advice of someone who knew it and then lost the hand but, although you will not win every hand, a person who follows proper "Basic Strategy" can easily achieve an almost break-even point against the house.

The Basic Strategy you will find in this book is FACT. Guesswork and intuition have no place in understanding the statistical significance of the "plays". Why this hand should be hit against this card etc. Basic Strategy is the correct way to play any possible hand in the game of Blackjack.

Basic Strategy can be broken down into five main categories.

1. Hard Hitting.
2. Soft Hitting.
3. Splitting Pairs.
4. Hard double downs.
5. Soft double downs.

1. Hard Hitting.

Your Hand	Dealer's Up Card
12	Hit against 2, 3 and 7 thru Ace. Otherwise Stand.
13, 14, 15, 16	Hit against 7 or higher. Otherwise Stand.
17, 18, 19, 20, 21	Always Stand.

2. Soft Hitting.

Your Hand	Dealer's Up Card
A-2, A-3, A-4, A-5, A-6	Always Hit, except when you can double down. (See 5).
A-7	Hit against a 9, 10 or Ace. Against a 2, 7 or 8 Stand. Otherwise double down.
A-8, A-9	Always Stand.

3. Splitting Pairs.

Your Hand	Dealer's Up Card
2-2, 3-3	7 or less Split.
4-4	5 or 6 Split.
6-6	6 or less Split.
7-7	7 or less Split.
8-8, A-A	Always Split.
9-9	2 to 6 and 8, 9 Split.
	(Not against 7)

Note: Always split 8's and Aces.

Never split 5's or 10's.

4. Hard double downs.

Your Hand	Dealer's Up Card
9	3 thru 6 Double.
10	9 or less Double.
11	10 or less Double.

5. Soft double downs.

Your Hand	Dealer's Up Card
A-2, A-3	5 or 6 Double.
A-4, A-5	4, 5, or 6 Double.
A-6, A-7	3, 4, 5 or 6 Double.

Practice.

Before you go further into this book you must have basic strategy completely memorized. No guessing whether or not to hit, stand or double down. You must know <u>exactly</u> what to do in all circumstances. All card counting techniques I will show you as we progress are centered around basic strategy. To try to learn too much before you are ready will only serve to confuse.

To help you learn faster and more efficiently I have included some practice charts. Use them as much as possible. When you can work your way through the last practice chart making your decision instantly, without hesitation and without mistakes. Only then are you ready to continue.

Remember, <u>Do Not Guess.</u> It is important that you learn basic strategy perfectly.

Practice 1. Hitting and Standing.

This chart shows all the troublesome hands for hitting or standing. Work your way through them one at a time asking yourself what you would do with this hand. For instance, your hand is a 9 and a 6, (15), against the dealer's 6. Do you hit or stand.

Use the basic strategy chart on page 39 to help. When you can get them all correct move to the next practice.

Your Hand	Dealer's Card	Your Hand	Dealer's Card	Your Hand	Dealer's Card
16	5	12	6	12	2
17	7	13	5	13	3
12	4	A-8	9	15	6
16	9	17	9	13	4
14	2	12	3	A-7	10
13	2	14	3	16	7

Practice 2. Splitting Pairs.

This next chart shows you all the possible hands to split. Again, work your way through them, one at a time, asking yourself yes or no. For instance, you have 8-8 against the dealer's 6. Do I split? Keep using the chart to help until you are completely confident with yourself.

Your Hand	Dealer Card	Your Hand	Dealer Card	Your Hand	Dealer Card	Your Hand	Dealer Card
9-9	8	8-8	A	A-A	A	2-2	10
9-9	A	2-2	3	4-4	6	3-3	5
3-3	4	4-4	4	8-8	2	7-7	10
2-2	6	8-8	10	3-3	10	A-A	9
2-2	2	7-7	4	2-2	8	7-7	3
7-7	2	9-9	7	8-8	6	10-10	5
2-2	4	9-9	2	6-6	7	9-9	9
6-6	2	6-6	6	9-9	10	7-7	5
9-9	6	3-3	3	7-7	7	6-6	3
7-7	10	A-A	2	3-3	7	4-4	7
5-5	5	6-6	4	3-3	2	A-A	6
		5-5	6	A-A	10		

Practice 3. Double Down.

This chart gives all the possible double down hands you may come across. Once more work through the chart asking yourself, do I double? Yes or no?

Your Hand	Dealer Card	Your Hand	Dealer Card	Your Hand	Dealer Card	Your Hand	Dealer Card
A-6	7	9	6	A-4	2	A-4	3
11	2	A-8	3	8	6	9	5
A-3	5	A-5	2	A-2	7	11	10
9	2	A-7	8	A-8	4	A-4	7
A-7	3	11	A	A-6	4	A-7	7
A-5	5	A-4	4	11	9	A-5	6
10	10	A-8	6	A-7	2	A-3	6
A-8	8	A-6	2	9	9	A-2	6
10	A	A-8	2	10	11	9	3
A-4	5	A-4	6	A-5	7	A-6	6
A-2	4	9	7	10	5	A-8	9
10	6	A-8	9	A-5	4	A-3	4
		9	8	10	2		

Practice 4. Problem Hands.

All the problem hands you will ever see are contained in this final chart. Keep practicing until you can complete the entire page without hesitation.

Remember, <u>Do Not Guess!</u> Use the basic strategy chart to help you if you are unsure. Once you can answer each and every one instantly and correctly you may congratulate yourself. You are now a master of basic strategy. This will now be your framework to the entire game. You are now ready to add to your knowledge some of the many count systems available. But it is important that you keep practicing. All or most of the card counting techniques revolve around basic strategy. You will continue to use it most of the time.

Practice 4.

Your Hand	Dealer Card	Your Hand	Dealer Card	Your Hand	Dealer Card	Your Hand	Dealer Card
16	2	A-2	6	5-5	2	A-A	2
8	5	13	3	3-3	5	A-4	4
4-4	3	14	5	12	6	A-A	3
14	2	10	9	4-4	6	13	8
2-2	2	6-6	4	15	3	4-4	4
15	A	9-9	5	A-5	4	11	8
A-8	5	3-3	6	A-7	2	13	10
A-A	10	15	5	3-3	3	A-6	6
8	4	14	3	A-7	10	12	3
A-4	5	10	4	A-A	3	13	5
3-3	7	A-6	4	15	2	8	3
12	5	A-2	3	10	5	A-A	A
14	4	3-3	4	A-7	3	A-9	6
4-4	5	15	6	A-6	10	12	2
A-2	4	10	3	A-A	9	13	6
3-3	8	A-6	2	4-4	4	16	5
5-5	7	2-2	4	A-8	3	6-6	6

36

Practice 4. Continued

Your Hand	Dealer Card	Your Hand	Dealer Card	Your Hand	Dealer Card	Your Hand	Dealer Card
9	4	A-3	3	16	8	4-4	7
A-2	5	13	2	10	8	A-A	8
14	6	3-3	2	A-6	5	8-8	9
15	4	16	3	7-7	6	11	5
A-9	3	9-9	A	13	A	7-7	2
A-9	5	11	2	14	A	7-7	5
9-9	3	A-5	3	16	4	14	10
16	9	7-7	8	9-9	6	11	3
A-7	5	10	6	A-8	2	2-2	5
6-6	3	A-3	4	14	7	9	5
11	9	2-2	6	A-5	6	15	7
9	8	9	7	A-3	5	16	10
A-7	4	9-9	2	A-7	A	15	9
11	4	2-2	8	8-8	10	9	3
2-2	8	6-6	7	9	8	A-5	6

Practice 4. Continued

Your Hand	Dealer Card	Your Hand	Dealer Card	Your Hand	Dealer Card	Your Hand	Dealer Card
15	7	A-9	6	A-9	6	9-9	4
16	6	7-7	8	16	A	11	6
10	A	2-2	3	9	2	15	8
A-9	4	6-6	5	A-3	6	A-4	2
6-6	2	A-8	6	2-2	7	A-9	4
16	7	15	10	7-7	4	11	10
14	9	9-9	7	A-7	6	8	3

Basic Strategy Chart.

X	2	3	4	5	6	7	8	9	10	A
9	H	D	D	D	D	H	H	H	H	H
10	D	D	D	D	D	D	D	D	H	H
11	D	D	D	D	D	D	D	D	D	H
12	H	H	S	S	S	H	H	H	H	H
13	S	S	S	S	S	H	H	H	H	H
14	S	S	S	S	S	H	H	H	H	H
15	S	S	S	S	S	H	H	H	H	H
16	S	S	S	S	S	H	H	H	H	H
2-2	Sp	Sp	Sp	Sp	Sp	Sp	H	H	H	H
3-3	Sp	Sp	Sp	Sp	Sp	Sp	H	H	H	H
4-4	H	H	H	Sp	Sp	H	H	H	H	H
6-6	Sp	Sp	Sp	Sp	Sp	H	H	H	H	H
7-7	Sp	Sp	Sp	Sp	Sp	Sp	H	H	H	H
8-8	Sp	Sp	Sp	Sp	Sp	Sp	Sp	Sp	Sp	Sp
9-9	Sp	Sp	Sp	Sp	Sp	S	Sp	Sp	S	S
A-A	Sp	Sp	Sp	Sp	Sp	Sp	Sp	Sp	Sp	Sp
A-2	H	H	H	D	D	H	H	H	H	H
A-3	H	H	H	D	D	H	H	H	H	H
A-4	H	H	D	D	D	H	H	H	H	H
A-5	H	H	D	D	D	H	H	H	H	H
A-6	H	D	D	D	D	H	H	H	H	H
A-7	S	D	D	D	D	S	S	H	H	H

H = HIT   S = STAND   D = DOUBLE DOWN   Sp = SPLIT

Blackjack Bloopers.

Having spent many years behind the tables I have seen countless players almost throwing away their hard earned money by making some of the worst mistakes possible. These are mistakes that the casino management love to see as it is easy money in their pockets. Although there are innumerable ways in which to fall into the waiting arms of the casino these are probably the top seven of the worst Blackjack bloopers you can make.

1. Splitting Tens.

The only time you would ever consider splitting tens is if you are either counting cards, have a plus count, and know it is to your advantage. Or in tournament play where you need to be more aggressive in order to get ahead quickly, but even then only against a dealer's 5 or 6. At any other time, Stand. You have 20 and a potential winner. If you split and get just one bad card you have turned that win into a push. If you get two low cards such as a 5 or 6 then the chances are that you will now lose both hands and twice the money. 20 will be a winner most of the time. Leave it alone!

2. Not Splitting Aces.

You *ALWAYS split* Aces. Even against a Ten or Ace. You are starting out with 2 or a soft 12. If you are up against a high card you have a potential loser in this state. You Split them up and you essentially now have two 11's. You get one ten and you are almost guaranteed a push. You get two 10's and you are practically home free. Now don't get me wrong. It won't work every time. Sometimes you will get 4's and 5's but the odds are most definitely in your favor to split. If you split and get another Ace and are

41

fortunate enough to be in a casino that will let you split Aces more than once, *DO IT.* The same rules apply.

3. Standing On A Soft Total.

Almost every day I see players who will stand on a soft 16 or a soft 15, (A-5 or A-4). You have absolutely nothing to lose and everything to gain by hitting these soft hands. If you hit and get a large card you hand is no worse off but if you get a small card your hand, and your chances of winning, have improved.

You have a soft 18, (Ace-7), against the dealer's 6 so you stand. You already have him beat so why risk changing the hand? When the dealer is showing a 5 or 6 the odds of him not making a hand are huge. Anything you can do to put up more money against him is in your best interests, (within reason of course, you still would never split 10's).

With a soft 17 or 18, (Ace-6 or Ace-7), you should double down your hand against the dealer's 3, 4, 5 or 6. If you get an Ace, two or three, (and with soft 17 a four), you have improved your hand. If you get a Ten, Jack, Queen or King the hand remains the same. If you get any of the remaining cards, 5 6 7 8 9, yes your hand is lower, but remember you are betting against the bad card the dealer is showing. Chances are he will go over.

Now if the dealer has a high card showing, (10 J Q K A), 17 and 18 are potential losers. If the dealer's hole card is a 9 or greater you have already lost, anything else and he still gets another shot. You must try to improve your hand and hit, if you get a low card your hand improves and you have a chance of survival but if you go over, with a soft total you get another try.

With a soft 18 against a 7, 8 or 9 stand. Against a high card hit, against a low card double.

43

Never stand on a soft 17. The main advantages you have as a player over the house are doubles and splits. Grab them!

4. Doubling Down For Less.

Most casinos will let you double down on your bet for less money than the original wager. If you double for less you are taking all of the risk by only getting one card but only receiving a portion of the reward if you win. One of the main advantages the player has over the casino is the ability to double down or split. If the odds are enough in your favor to allow you to double your bet grab the chance while you can.

5. Hitting Against The Dealer's Bust Card.

This is a common mistake among beginner Blackjack players and where the casino gains most of its edge over you. If you get 18 and the dealer gets 18 it's a "push". Nobody wins or loses. If you get 20 and the dealer gets 20 it's a push. But if you go over and the dealer goes over the house wins. The catch is, you go first. If the dealer has a low card, 6 or less, don't risk it. Your best odds are to Stand on 12 or above and let them take the bust card. Keep in mind, you don't have to get 21, just beat the dealer.

6. Not Hitting A Hand Because You Have A Large Number Of Cards.

I see many players who start with a low hand, let's say 5. They hit and get a 3, hit again, get another 3, hit again and receive a 2, then another 3. Now they have 16 against a high card, (7 thru 10), but won't hit, simply because they already have five cards. "The next card has to be a 10 and I'll bust right?" Wrong! The odds remain the same. Whether you have two, five or even eight cards, you still have 16 against a high card and a potential loser. You must hit to try to improve the hand.

7. Not Splitting Eights.

A pair of eights is where many players seem to fall by the wayside. Splitting eights against a small card is always attractive but when faced with a dealer's 10 or Ace the decision can become more intimidating. Fearing the end result of two 18's against a 20 many players will take the unfavorable decision to hit. I could now go into an endless stream of figures and percentages of why this is the wrong decision but that would take far too long. The short and the tall of it is that 16 against a high card, (7 through Ace), is a potential losing hand. Hitting the 16 may bring the happy arrival of a four or five but that is unlikely. The reasoning behind splitting eights against a high card is to turn that potential loser into a push. You are trying to save the hand.

If after you split you get a 2 or 3 you now have an attractive double down hand and a likely winner. If you receive a 10, Jack, Queen, King or Ace you have a good hand and a reasonable chance of survival. If you are given a low card you are really no worse off than before, and the likelihood of this happening to both hands is small. If given another eight the above still applies. Hard as it may be, split them again.

Follow this "golden rule" and no matter what the dealer's up card may be always split eights. Keep in mind that you will lose your fair share of these splits but if you were to hit or stand you would be losing more money in the long term.

As I stated earlier, these are probably some of the worst mistakes you can make on the tables, and they will cost you.

Always keep in mind that the casino is there to make money - YOURS.

Money Management.

While gambling in a casino money management is probably the most important key to success. Without proper control over your bankroll you will more than likely end up losing. First some common sense rules. It is very important that you bet within your means. Do not play with money you cannot afford to lose and never, never chase your losses. If you have a bad run it can sometimes be difficult to control your temper. If you feel this happening to you then <u>walk away</u>. Take some time out to relax and gather your emotions before returning to the tables. It is important that you remain calm and in control while playing otherwise you are likely to make mistakes and end up throwing good money after bad.

There are many different betting systems a Blackjack player could adopt. Some are beneficial while others are a sure recipe for disaster. Here are a few examples of money management systems.

Flat Betting.

Flat Betting is making the same wager every hand regardless of win or loss. With the "house" having an advantage of anywhere between one and five percent, playing this way you may get lucky from time to time but eventually the odds will catch up to you. Over the course of time you can only lose.

Lose Press.

The Lose Press system, also known as the martingale system, is to flat bet while you are winning but whenever you lose you double your bet. Starting with $10 if you lose you bet $20. Lose again bet $40, next $80 then $160 and so on until, when you eventually win, you return to your flat bet of $10.

$10	Lose	$25	Lose
$20	Lose	$50	Lose
$40	Lose	$100	Lose
$80	Win	$200	Win
$10	---	$25	---

The general idea behind this system is that sooner or later you have to win a hand. Unfortunately as you can see you can end up betting a huge amount of money in a very short period of time, ($540 after just six losses), in order to recoup your original flat bet of $10. Also if you are playing on a game with a $500 maximum bet, after losing six hands in a row you will have no hope of recovery. This is one of the reasons why the house imposes a maximum bet on the game.

Win Press.

Press your bet by one unit every time you win. Starting with your flat bet of one unit, you win once, bet two units. Once again bet three. Win again take it to four, then five, six and so on. You are only at risk on your first two hands, after that you are betting entirely with the casino's money. Take it as high as you can go. When you lose go back to one unit. The only down side with this system is on Blackjack, where you can get your bet up high but then need to double or split. Now it's make or break time. You can end up risking everything you've worked for the last hour on just one hand.

$10	Win		$25	Win
$20	Win		$50	Win
$30	Win		$75	Win
$40	Lose		$100	Lose
$10	---		$25	---

Double Win Press.

To Double Win Press you bet the total amount won. If your original bet is one unit, you win the next hand and now bet two. Another win bet four. Successful again takes you to eight. You should set yourself a limit as to how high you are willing to press as you win nothing until you start pulling back your money. Once you lose a hand return to your original bet.

$10	Win	$25	Win
$20	Win	$50	Win
$40	Win	$100	Win
$80	Lose	$200	Lose
$10	---	$25	---

Power Press.

Power Pressing is increasing your bet with the amount won and adding to it from your bankroll.

You bet one unit on the first hand and win, then bet three. Win again and increase to eight. Another win takes you to twenty units. Once you lose a bet return to your original wager. How much money you are willing to take out of your bankroll depends upon how aggressive you wish to be.

Remember, until you start pulling money back from your bet you have won nothing.

$10	Win	$25	Win
$30	Win	$75	Win
$80	Win	$200	Win
$200	Lose	$500	Lose
$10	---	$25	---

If you can get ahead early by win pressing you can be extremely difficult for the house to beat. Unless you bet hunches and power press you are wagering with the casino's money and not your own bankroll. You must lose consistently in order to be beaten. Win press players who manage their bankroll the best are those who remove money from the bet as the run progresses, thereby increasing their winnings.

D'Alembert.

This is a simple linear system named after the eighteenth century theorist Jean le Rond d'Alembert. He mistakenly reasoned that if a coin landed on heads a number of times in a row, that tails was more likely to hit next time. In this system bearing his name you raise your bet by one unit if you lose and lower it by one unit if you win. Bet $10, lose and bet $20, win and bet $10, lose and bet $20, lose again and bet $30, lose once more, bet $40, win, bet $30, ad infinitum. The end result is likely to be the same - you lose.

Labouchere.

The Labouchere system, also known as the cancellation system, can be additive in nature. A sequence of numbers, for instance 1,2,3,4, is chosen. The first bet is the total of the two numbers on the end, or in this example 5 units. If the bet is lost then the lost bet now becomes the last number of the new sequence, 1,2,3,4,5. The next bet is now the sum of the new first and last numbers. In the above example, 6. If the bet is won, the first and last numbers in the sequence are canceled, in this case with the sequence 1,2,3,4, the 1 and 4 are canceled, and, the next bet is the sum of the two non-canceled numbers, 2 and 3. If you win, you proceed to the inside numbers until they are all canceled out. Again a loser, but an insidious one.

Card Counting Strategies.

Some people will tell you that counting cards is a myth. "Impossible" they say, "especially with four, six or even eight decks". "It can't be done!" they say. Counting cards can not only be done but it is also a relatively easy technique that can be learned by most in a matter of minutes. Anyone who can add together one and one and come up with two can learn how to count cards, it's that simple. All that is required is concentration, a little knowledge and a great deal of practice.

Card counting is the process of tracking cards as they are removed from the shoe and, believe it or not, the more decks the better. If the game is played with two decks and the dealer cuts off one deck that is half of the cards, 50%, you don't get to see. If the house is using six decks and cuts off one then the percentage of cards you don't get to see is now down to only 16.5%. You get to see 83.5% of the cards, thus giving you a much better advantage. Contrary to popular belief you do not have to have a photographic memory or possess a huge I.Q. to do this. All that is required is plenty of practice and the ability to keep your mind on the game at all times.

The game of Blackjack is based upon percentages with the house will having at any given time a two to five percent advantage over the player. By playing perfect basic strategy you can reduce that to as low as one percent, but even then the house still has the edge, after all this is why they are there. What you now need to learn is how to turn that percentage to your favor, and this is where card counting comes in.

By knowing what percentage of large cards have been removed from the shoe you are able to establish the percentage of small cards remaining and vice-versa. This will give you a better idea of when to hit and stand and how much to bet at any given time. Your decisions will be based upon actual odds and not just gut feelings. Ultimately, you will profit more in Blackjack if you count cards.

For instance, if you have a 13 against the dealer's 4 and you know that there is a large amount of small cards left then you would hit the hand. With the deck being full of small cards the chances of the dealer making a hand is much greater. Similarly if you have a 10 against the dealer's 9, knowing that the shoe will offer mainly small cards, you would not double down. If you know that there is a large percentage of 10's or Aces left in the shoe then you have an enormous advantage. The richer the deck is in tens the better chance you have of winning, generally. Although the dealer could make a Blackjack hand just as easily as you, you get paid 3-2 whereas the dealer only gets even money. If you receive a bad hand you do not have to draw, the dealer does, and if the shoe is full of large cards the chances are he will probably go over. Also you can afford to be more aggressive, doubling on a 9 against a 7 or 8, doubling on A-9 against a 5 or 6 or even splitting 10's. As you can see, a good card counting technique can give a gambler a clear advantage over the casino.

There are a number of card counting systems in existence today. Some are fairly simple and easy to learn while others can be complex and take a great deal of time to perfect. The ratio between difficulty and practical application to their effectiveness can differ substantially. As shown here the harder and more complex systems are not necessarily the best.

Strategy	Increased Win Bets Per Hour	Difficulty
Wide range of numbers	.05	More memory
Counting 1/2's	.10	Harder
Counting Aces	.10	2 Counts
10 Count -Aces	.15	2 Running Counts
10 Count +Aces	.10	3 Running Counts
2 Card Combos	.05	Complex Tables

The following chart will show you a few examples of different counting techniques.

System	Card	2	3	4	5	6	7	8	9	T	A
Hi-Lo (+ / -)		+1	+1	+1	+1	+1	0	0	0	-1	-1
Revere PT CT		+1	+2	+2	+2	+2	+1	0	0	-2	-2
Revere Advanced		+1	+1	+1	+1	+1	0	0	-1	-1	0
Revere Advanced PT CT 71		+2	+3	+3	+4	+3	+2	0	-1	-3	-4
Revere Advanced PT CT 73		+2	+2	+3	+4	+1	+1	0	-2	-3	0
Gordon + / -		+1	+1	+1	+1	0	0	0	0	-1	0
Ten Count		+4	+4	+4	+4	+4	+4	+4	+4	-9	-4
Einstein HI-OPT		0	+1	+1	+1	+1	0	0	0	-1	0

The Knock-Out System.

The "Knock-Out" System was originally developed under the philosophy expressed by Albert Einstein that; "Everything should be as simple as possible, but not more so". Based upon this principle the Knock-Out is a single level, single parameter count system, designed to be highly effective while using a bare minimum of Basic Strategy changes, (if any). Most importantly the Knock-Out system's unbalanced nature can completely eliminate the necessity to convert to a true count. We'll get to that in a moment.

First, we must be able to do the required counting, which means we need to be able to recognize which cards, as they leave the game, will help us or hurt us. It turns out that as the little cards, (2 thru 7), are removed our expectation of winning

63

goes up. On the other hand, as the big cards, (10, J, Q, K, A), are played our expectations go down. The middle cards, (8 and 9), are neutral, and have little effect either way.

$$2, 3, 4, 5, 6, 7 = +1 \quad \text{(24 total points)}$$
$$8, 9 = 0$$
$$10, J, Q, K, Ace = -1 \quad \text{(20 total points)}$$

Notice that there are more points on the plus side, (+), than on the minus, (-). Because these totals do not even out the Knock-Out system is referred to as "unbalanced". It is this unbalanced aspect that sets the Knock-Out count apart from its balanced predecessors. It is also the unbalanced nature of the count that eliminates the need to make the brutal true-count conversions. We keep only the running count for all betting and strategy decisions.

So how does it work? Let's use an example from the single-deck game to demonstrate.

After the shuffle start with an initial running count of zero. Then just add or subtract, as applicable, according to the cards that are played. Easy enough, but how do we know when we have the advantage? Simple. The count indicates that the deck favors us when we reach a point that we call the key count. Any time the count is at or above the key count before a hand, we generally have the advantage. The higher the count goes, the greater our advantage is likely to be. In a single-deck game the key count is +2.

Armed with this information, (and Basic Strategy), we now bet more when we have the advantage, (the count is at +2 or more), and only a little when the house has the advantage, (the count is below +2). Believe it or not, mastery of this simple plan is sufficient enough to beat the casino's at the single-deck game, while with slight modifications, the Knock-Out can also identify when the player has the advantage in multiple-deck games.

It's important to note that I have not suggested that you vary the play of the hands from Basic Strategy. In fact, simply betting higher with the advantage can generally account for 70% to 90% of the value of a card-counting system. The remaining profit comes from varying strategy as dictated by the remaining deck composition.

Once you are comfortable counting and betting accordingly, you may wish to add some Knock-Out clout by using a few of the variation plays, (based on the count), to further increase your advantage. One of the most valuable of these plays is Insurance.

Remember that insurance is offered to players when the dealer has an Ace showing. It is really a side wager on whether or not the dealer has a 10 in the hole. A Basic Strategy player would never take insurance, but we are card counters! We should take insurance if there is an appropriate majority of tens remaining in the deck. Knock-Out allows us to accurately identify these situations in a simple way, (the insurance running count value, as in the Hi-Lo system is +3), again without the need for converting to a true count.

Similarly, some of the other variation plays may be added at your leisure, each one relying only on the running count.

Hi - Lo.

The Hi - Lo system, also known as the Plus - Minus (+ / -) system, is probably one of the easiest counting techniques to learn and yet one of the most efficient. Keeping track of the cards is much easier than you would think. Each card is assigned a point value. Plus one, (+1), minus one, (-1), or zero, (0). With just a few minutes of practice you will easily be able to keep track of the cards. The entire Hi - Lo strategy can be learned by most people in just a few days.

The Running Count.

Tracking the cards with the following point values will determine the "Running Count".

Card	Value
2 3 4 5 6	+1
7 8 9	0
10 J Q K A	-1

The running count is the sum of how many more high or low cards are remaining in the shoe. This is determined by mentally adding and subtracting the value of each card as it is dealt.

Begin your count as each player receives his/her second card and total one hand at a time. This will enable you to use a technique known as canceling. If you have both a plus and a minus card in one hand they cancel each other out and you can save time by ignoring this particular hand. Count the dealer's up card and all following hit cards as they are dealt.

These cards have a value of +1 each.

These cards have a value of -1 each.

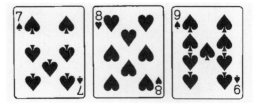

These cards have a value of 0.

Practice 1.

Take a single deck of cards and turn them over one at a time mentally keeping a running count. At the end of the deck your final total should be 0.

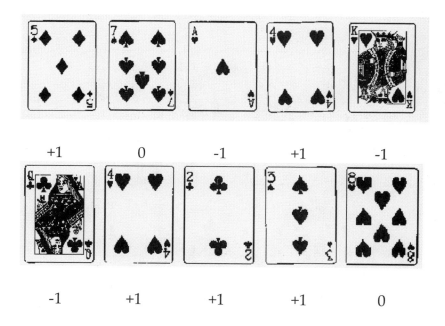

The running count after these cards is +2.

If you like you can remove one card from the deck and, without looking, place it face down. After working through the deck your final count total should tell you the value of the card.

Practice 2.

Do as before but this time turn two cards at a time. Practice canceling out.

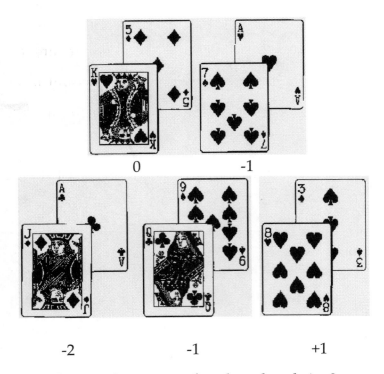

0   -1

-2   -1   +1

The running count after these hands is -3.

The True Count.

After establishing the running count you must then determine the "True Count". The true count is the figure around which all your decisions shall be made. Finding the true count is the process of determining what the count is per deck, (52 cards). A running count of +4 is not that good if there are five decks left to be dealt, but if you have a +4 count while only one deck remains this puts you in a very advantageous position.

To determine the true count you must divide the running count by the amount of decks remaining in the shoe. For instance if the running count is +6 and there are two decks left, (6 divided by 2 is 3), your true count is +3. The amount of each bet or any decisions regarding the play of the hand must be based upon the true count.

To determine the number of decks remaining in the shoe estimate the number of decks in the discard rack. Each deck is approximately 3/4 inch. Subtract that amount from the number of decks being used, usually either four, six or eight decks, and that will give you the number of decks remaining.

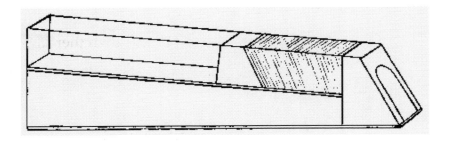

6 Deck Shoe

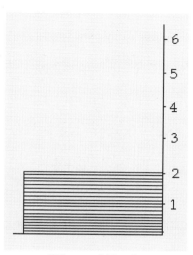

6

5

4

3

2

1

Discard Rack

If two decks are in the discard holder then there are

four decks remaining in play.

Running count is +12.

Number of decks remaining is 4.

True Count is +3.

Variations From Basic Strategy.

Now that you know how to determine the true

count you must now learn how to determine when it

would be appropriate to make a play that is contrary

to basic strategy. For example if you have A-9 against the dealer's 6 you would normally stand, but if you have a count of true +1 then you know that there is a higher than average percentage of high cards left in the shoe, so now you would double down.

Similarly if you have 14 against a 2 and you have a true count of -4, knowing that there is now a higher percentage of small cards remaining you would hit.

The following chart, (on page 67), will show you when to deviate from basic strategy and when not. All numbers shown are true count.

Although all the variations in this chart are of importance there are some that you are very unlikely to need. For instance, with a true count of +23 you would double down on a 7 against the dealer's 2, however it is extremely rare for a true count to reach that high.

Variation Chart - Hi-Lo.

X	2	3	4	5	6	7	8	9	10	A
12	+3 S	+2 S	-1 H	-2 H	-1 H					
13	-1 H	-2 H	-4 H	-5 H	-5 H					
14	-4 H	-5 H	-7 H	-8 H	-8 H					
15	-6 H	-7 H	-8 H	-10 H	-10 H	+10 S	-8 S	+4 S	+10 S	
16	-9 H	-11 H	-12 H	-13 H	-14 H	+8 S	-7 S	+5 S	+1 S	+8 S
17										
2-2	-4 H	-6 H	-8 H	-10 H	-13 H	-28 H	+5 H			
3-3	-1 H	-5 H	-8 H	-10 H	-14 H	-29 H	+4 Sp			
4-4	+15 Sp	+6 Sp	+1 Sp	-2 H	-5 H					
6-6	-2 H	-5 H	-7 H	-9 H	-11 H					
7-7	-10 H	-12 H	-14 H	-15 H	-21 H	-28 H	+5 Sp			
8-8								+8 S		
9-9	-3 S	-4 S	-6 S	-7 S	-7 S	+3 Sp	-9 S	-10 S		+3 Sp
10-10	-11 Sp	-8 Sp	+6 Sp	+5 Sp	+4 Sp					
A-A	-12 H	-13 H	-13 H	-14 H	-15 H	-10 H	-9 H	-8 H	-9 H	-4 H
7	+23 D	+16 D	+12 D	+9 D	+9 D					
8	+13 D	+9 D	-5 D	+3 D	+1 D	+14 D				
9	+1 D	-1 H	-3 H	-5 H	-7 H	+3 D	+7 D			
10	-9 H	-10 H	-11 H	-12 H	-14 H	-7 H	-5 H	-2 H	+4 D	+4 D
11	-12 H	-13 H	-13 H	-14 H	-15 H	-10 H	-7 H	-5 H	-5 H	+1 D
A-2	+13 D	+7 D	+3 D	-1 H	-2 H					
A-3	+14 D	+7 D	+1 D	-2 H	-5 H					
A-4	+18 D	+7 D	-1 H	-5 H	-10 H					
A-5	+15 D	+4 D	-3 H	-7 H	-13 H					
A-6	+1 D	-4 H	-8 H	-11 H	-14 H					
A-7	+1 D	-3 S	-7 S	-9 S	-11 S					
A-8	+8 D	+5 D	+3 D	+1 D	+1 D					
A-9	+10 D	+8 D	+6 D	+5 D	+4 D					

TAKE INSURANCE ON +3 OR MORE

Below is a list of the most important variation plays. They are listed in order of importance. Take the time to memorize these plays perfectly as these are the ones you will most need.

Your Hand	Dealer's Up Card	True Count	Decision
Insurance	Any	+3	Take Insurance
16	10	+1	Stand
15	10	+4	Stand
10-10	5	+5	Split
10-10	6	+4	Split
10	10	+4	Double down
12	3	+2	Stand
12	2	+3	Stand
11	A	+1	Double down
9	2	+1	Double down
10	A	+4	Double down
9	7	+3	Double down
16	9	+5	Stand
13	2	-1	Hit
12	4	-1	Hit
12	5	-2	Hit
12	6	-1	Hit
13	3	-2	Hit

Insurance.

The <u>only</u> time you should ever take insurance is when the true count is +3 or higher, regardless of your hand.

Surrender.

Some casinos will offer you the option to "surrender" your hand, giving up half of your bet as an "easy out" on a bad hand. Normally you would not consider this but, while counting, you have an advantage. Having 16 in your hand against the dealer's 10 is a bad situation at the best of times, but if you know that there is a large percentage of small cards remaining in the shoe then you now have a better chance of making a hand. Similarly if you have a high plus count, telling you that the shoe is now rich in large cards, you have little hope for success. This is when surrender suddenly becomes more attractive.

The higher the true count the more you will surrender.

Below is a list of all the surrender plays. These are the only times that surrender should be taken.

Your Hand	Dealer's Up Card	True Count
16	A	+1
16	10	+1
16	9	+2
16	8	+4
15	A	+1
15	10	+1
15	9	+2
14	A	+3

Money Management 2.

Of all the areas in which you are required to perform in order to employ a successful card counting technique money management is probably the most abused. Whether it is boredom, greed, ignorance, impatience or just being too much of a gambler, more card counters go down to defeat because of over-betting their bankroll than any other reason. It is important that you always bet in proportion with the money you have. This will help to increase your advantage. Do not play with money you cannot afford and never exceed your bankroll.

To make money counting cards you must vary your bet size by at least five "units". If your minimum bet is $10 then your maximum bet would be $50. If your minimum bet is $25 then you would never bet higher than $125. As a bankroll you need to

81

carry five times your maximum bet. For example if your maximum bet is $50 you will need a bankroll of $250. If your maximum bet is $125 then your bankroll must be $750.

Minimum Bet	$10	$25	1 Unit
	$20	$50	2 Units
	$30	$75	3 Units
	$40	$100	4 Units
Maximum Bet	$50	$125	5 Units

Although it sometimes may be tempting it is important that you never exceed your maximum bet. Even if the count is with you it is still possible to lose a hand. You do not want to have hours of work wiped out by a single hand.

As you can see from the following chart, a shoe does not become profitable until the count reaches true +2, and any bet made upon a minus count is a losing proposition. When the count is minus bet either table minimum or nothing at all. The higher the plus count the better your advantage, so your bets should be made accordingly.

True Count	Player's Win Percentage
-2	-1.50
-1	-1.00
0	-0.45
+1	+0.10
+2	+0.50
+3	+1.40
+4	+2.40
+5	+3.60
+6	+5.40
+7	+7.50
+8	+9.80

ven or minus count bet 1 Unit. (Minimum bet)

On a true +1 bet 2 Units.

On a true +2 bet 3 Units.

On a true +3 bet 4 Units.

On a true +4 or more bet 5 Units. (Maximum bet).

The techniques you have now learned need to be applied at every opportunity. Keep practicing until you are confident and comfortable with your abilities. Even though you have now learned the Hi-Lo count system you must still keep practicing basic strategy. Any mistakes you make while playing the game is money you are losing.

Practice.

Use the following chart to help practice everything you have now learned. In this chart you will be given the running count and the number of decks remaining in the shoe. You must calculate the true count and decide how much your wager on each hand would be given that you are betting in $25 units. For example the running count is +4 and there are two decks left in the shoe. This gives you a true count of +2 and you would bet three units or $75.

Running Count	Decks Remaining	True Count	Your Bet
+4	2	**+2**	**$75**

Next you must make a decision on your hand according to the true count. If, as above, your true count is +2 then you know there is a large percentage of high cards remaining. Therefore if you have 16 against the dealer's 10 you would stand.

Your Hand	Dealer's Up Card	Decision
16	10	**Stand**

Work your way through the practice one line at a time. Use the charts to help. When you can

complete the entire chart with no mistakes you are
ready to play.

Practice.

Running Count	Decks Remaining	True Count	Your Bet	Your Hand	Dealer's Card	Decision
+1	6			11	A	
+2	2			16	10	
-2	3			12	4	
-10	2			A-A	A	
+6	2			12	3	
-4	4			12	4	
+8	2			10-10	5	
+9	3			A-9	6	
-3	2			13	2	
+6	3			8	5	
-2	1			12	6	
-7	3			A-2	6	
+12	1			15	9	
+1	1			A-7	2	

Casual Card Counting.

So that's how you count cards. Yes, it can take a little bit of concentration and that may take away some of the enjoyment of playing the game. However, you may also choose to use a "casual" card counting system, which is much easier to master.

Casual card counting is just that, casual. It doesn't take a lot of concentration or mathematical calculations and demands very little use of your memory. You already know that a deck rich in face cards is an advantage to the player. Now all you need to do is casually observe the flow of cards coming out of a deck or shoe watching for "clumps". For example, if you are playing a multiple deck shoe and after a few hands you observe that very few face cards or Aces were played you have a situation where

87

the next hand will probably be good for the player, this is when you could increase your bet.

The key to this system is to look for extremes. The absence or predominance of exposed high cards is easily noticeable by casual observation. Often you will play several hands where the mix of face cards and low value cards are relatively even. But when you see a noticeable absence of high value cards you should increase your next wager.

Casual card counting is something you should always do unless you are following a strict card counting system such as the Hi-Lo system. It won't guarantee winners for you on every hand, but it will give you a slight advantage.

Cover Play.

Although counting cards is completely legal, (as long as you are not using any kind of mechanical means), most casino's simply don't like it and will do as much as possible to deter you. It is in their interests to know exactly where the percentages lie. They also know that, as a card counter, you have the ability to sway those percentages to your advantage. The house sees this as a potential threat. They know that the longer you play in their casino the higher the probability is that you will win.

<u>Probability of Winning</u>

After 5 hours of play	62%
After 20 hours of play	73%
After 100 hours of play	92%
After 400 hours of play	**99%**

While card counting is not illegal in any state or country it is a proven fact that an effective card counting technique can give an "unfair advantage," as the casinos call it, to the Blackjack player thus putting the house in a disadvantageous position because it's a highly specialized skill against which there is practically no known defense.

Some casinos do not seem overly concerned in this respect but there are many who employ a well trained supervisory staff who are taught to recognize "unusual play". These casinos will have brought together a group of specially trained individuals. A "Count Team". Usually Supervisors or Pit Bosses who have the ability to identify a card counter and can take measures that can make it difficult for you to win. These measures could include any of the following:

1. **Limit you to playing only one hand at a time.**

2. **Reduce the table maximum to $100 or less.**

   If you are betting in units of $50 or more this can make it difficult for you to continue.

3. **Cut the shoe in half.**

   This is probably one of the casino's most effective weapons against you. You would have to have a huge running count right at the start in order to make any kind of headway.

4. **No Comps.**

   They will do whatever they feel necessary to discourage your business or just generally make you feel unwelcome.

5. **Shuffle.**

   A member of their count team may be watching, counting the shoe along with you.

When the count reaches a large plus count, usually +2 or more, they will tell the dealer to shuffle. Sometimes they will even use your bet as a guideline and when you put up a large amount they will shuffle.

6.   **Eviction.**

In some extreme circumstances it is possible that the management may ask you to leave and/or bar you from further play at their casino. Take note that if this was to happen, most likely your picture will be sent to other casinos and you may experience problems playing elsewhere.

To be successful in counting cards you need to remain undetected. In order to do so you may at times have to employ slightly different methods of play. This is known as camouflage or "Cover Play".

If you have any reason to believe that you are being watched more closely than usual, or that a supervisor or pit boss seems to be constantly staring at your table or another supervisor suddenly appears, maybe with pencil and paper, then this is when you would bring cover play into effect. What these people are most likely doing is "running down the shoe". They will count the deck while checking out your play, watching to see how you will react to a large plus or minus count or if you play any variations. Standing on a 16 against a 10 is a dead giveaway. To throw them off you need to make a few little "mistakes". Cover Play. Bet flat bets, raising and dropping a unit now and then or maybe even adopt a win press system. Don't do anything too obvious such as splitting 10's as this is likely to let them know that you are smart enough to catch them watching you. What you need them to think is that you are just another dumb Blackjack player who isn't really sure of what he is doing. Some good cover plays are as follows.

Surrender on 12 thru 16 against a 9, 10 or Ace.

Double down on 10 against a 10 or Ace.

Bet big on the first hand of the shoe.

Double down on 11 against an Ace.

Buy Insurance.

Do Not Change your splitting strategies.

These subtle "mistakes" should satisfy the house that you are not counting. How could you be with all these slip-ups? Keep playing cover for a few minutes after you see them leave or at least until the end of the shoe, and then return to normal play.

It is very important nowadays to put on a good act and to be careful how you bet. This is especially the case if you are a green or black chip player. Pit Bosses know that a large bettor can obviously win more than a small bettor so they will tend to focus more of their attention on players who make bigger bets. If you are betting large units, $50 or more, try not to have too large of an amount sitting on the table in front of you as this obvious show of wealth is sure to bring the unwelcome attention of the Pit Boss. Don't give them a reason to check you out.

Shuffle Tracking.

The idea itself behind "shuffle tracking" is relatively simple. Imagine you are sitting at a Blackjack game watching the count climb slowly higher and higher until, just when it reaches what seems must be a record high, out comes the cut card. Sadly, you stare at that one deck remaining. That small portion which must contain more than a quarter of the tens and Aces in the shoe. Woefully, you continue watching the dealer as he stacks the cut-offs on top of the deck to begin his shuffle procedure and, to your amazement, when he has finish the shuffle and hands you the cut card you are still staring at that small group of cards.

Hard as it is to believe, that little group of cards, now only slightly dispersed, is sitting just two decks down in the cards the dealer is offering you.

You take the cut card and gently slip it in just about where the "slug" starts. The dealer then cuts the cards and places them in the shoe with the slug right at the front and, for the next couple of minutes, the tens and Aces just pour out from the shoe.

Although shuffle tracking does not guarantee you a win, (you can still be the unlucky recipient of a 15 or 16 while everyone else gets 20's and Blackjacks), you still have some huge advantages.

It's just like having a large plus count right at the beginning of the shoe and, since the shoe has only just begun and the count will most likely be in the high minuses, you don't have to worry about employing cover play. You will be able to bet big right at the start of the shoe and, if you utilize a few variation plays or even take insurance on that 20, any Pit Boss watching will assume you are just a normal everyday Blackjack player.

Unlike typical card counting methods, shuffle tracking, when done correctly, is immediately apparent. The results are right in front of you. When you are card counting you will raise and lower your bet according to the count but the cards you are expecting don't always come out. They can be further down the shoe or even behind the cut card. With shuffle tracking the big cards will always come out. They have to come out because you know where they are.

Another version of tracking cards is a system known as "clumping". This is a very simple tactic involving only a little memory skills. Let's say that in the course of play you happen to notice a large group of tens and Aces all together on the table. Instead of trying to track this entire slug through the shuffle an easier way is to just memorize the next three cards after the group. For instance, the 3 of diamonds, the 5 of hearts and the 9 of clubs.

When the dealer picks up this group those three cards will be positioned on the top so, as they go through the shuffle procedure, they should remain on top causing them to exit the shoe just before your clump. When the next shoe begins you just keep an eye out for those three cards, the 3 of diamonds, the 5 of hearts and the 9 of clubs, in that order. There will more than likely be other cards interspersed with these, you are just looking for them to be close together. When this happens all those tens and Aces you saw should not be far behind.

It is important to note that this is not an exact science and that results can vary greatly from shuffle to shuffle, but it will give you a little help.

Casino Etiquette.

As with most things, around the game of Blackjack there has evolved a number of unwritten rules. Do's and don'ts of the game. Some of these are trivial and have little significance but there are some that, if not adhered to, could get an unsuspecting player into trouble. Here are a few examples of casino protocol which I feel to be important.

Don't Touch The Cards.

In any casino unless you are playing on a pitch game, moving or touching the cards will invoke some kind of response from the dealer. If you wish to split let the dealer know verbally and he/she will move the cards for you. Also don't touch your bet once the cards are out and the hand is in play. If you wish to know how much is there to split or double down ask the dealer. Once again they will do it for you.

100

Don't Drink To Excess.

Having one or two beers is fine but you have to remember that, just as in driving, alcohol impairs your judgment and affects your ability to concentrate. Stay sober.

Make Signals Clearly.

When making signals to the dealer for a hit or to stand be sure to make it as obvious as possible. Use your whole hand to either tap the table next to your cards for a hit or wave from side to side over your cards to stand. Any misunderstanding between you and the dealer could prove costly and, if it can be fixed, a supervisor or pit boss will be called to rectify the mistake bringing you unwelcome attention.

Don't Criticize The Play Of Others.

This is only likely to cause problems. Although you may mean well people will play the way they want to play and, in most cases, somebody telling them they are doing wrong will just irritate them and most probably start an argument. Let them split their 5's or stand on soft 16. It's their money. The fact is, the way other people play their hands does not in any way determine whether or not you will win or lose, neither will it influence the dealer's hand. The cards come out of the shoe in a completely random order, the sequence of which nobody could know. The fact that another player before you either does or does not take a card will not affect the odds of you either pulling a 5 on a 16 or getting an 8 to go with your 12. If the card is there then the card is there. Who's to say that he is not helping by removing a 10 before your much needed 5? The foolish or stupid plays by other players do not alter your long-term results. The flow of the cards may be altered, but the final results offset. You are just as likely to win a hand or lose a hand as the result of a player's "mistake" in play.

Even if they do take your advice, if they lose the hand while doing so they will automatically hold you responsible. By telling someone how to play you are placing yourself in a no-win situation.

Don't Blame The Dealer For Getting Bad Cards.

First of all it isn't their fault. The cards in the shoe are mixed thoroughly and are cut by a third party. All the dealer does is remove the cards from the deck and place them in front of you. He/she has no more idea than you as to what they will be, and it is your decision what to do with the hand when you get it. By taking your frustrations out on the dealer all you are achieving is to upset someone who is just doing their job, possibly causing them to make mistakes, while annoying other players at the table.

103

By remaining calm and friendly you will help maintain a positive attitude at the game. This will definitely make it easier for you to concentrate.

Tip The Dealer.

The dealer's, even though it may not seem so, do work hard. They put in long hours and work outrageous shifts and yet are usually paid only minimum wage. Tips make up approximately 60 to 80 percent of their wages and they rely upon them heavily. They have families to feed too. If the casino's had to pay a true living wage to dealers instead of dealers accepting tips, casino's would have to figure a way of making up for lost revenue. For starters, they would change the rules of the game, increase table minimums, and even alter paybacks.

In a restaurant people will typically give 10 to 15 percent for good service yet, when winning in a casino, they tend to forget. Rather than just giving the dealer the money you can also play it for them. Place it on the corner of the box next to your bet and play your hand as normal. Although it will not affect whether you win or lose it will increase the dealer's desire to see you win and create a friendly atmosphere at the game.

Never Leave Money/Chips Unattended.

You see it all the time. Mr. X needs the bathroom or has to make a telephone call so, at the end of the shoe, off he goes calling over his shoulder for the dealer to watch his chips for him. In some cases this can be thousands of dollars. This could prove to be a very expensive mistake. The dealer cannot leave the game. If someone were to pick up the money and leave all the dealer can do is call for help, and by the time it arrives the thief and the money are most often long gone. The house is not responsible for your money. Remember that in a casino you are surrounded by people who are losing or have lost their money. A bunch of chips sitting all alone presents an easy target for an opportunist. There are even some who will go out of their way to look for this chance. If for any reason you feel you have to leave the game take your money with you. If necessary the dealer will keep your place at the table for you.

Complimentaries.
The Value Of The Comp... Getting Your Share Of Free Stuff

Imagine that you have just arrived at one of the many casinos' now open in the United States and have decided to try your hand at Blackjack. While seating yourself at a likely table, you see another player hand a small plastic card to the dealer, who passes the card to their supervisor, who after copying the name and number returns it to the player. "What does the card do?" you ask. The player looks up and says, "It keeps track of my comps." Just what are "comps," and how do you get them?

Casino "Comps" or complimentaries, are rewards or "gifts" given to valued customers based on "rated play." Comps are offered to encourage regular repeat visits by high turnover, high denomination players.

Casino player rating systems are based on average bet, time played, and type of game played. A player tracking computer calculates comps based on a "theoretical win point system" that tells casino operators how valuable your play is to them. At the heart of the system is a player card, issued through a players club, which identifies you and is presented at the beginning of your play. Player cards can come in different levels: VIP, Gold, Member, etc. Comps are awarded based on a certain percentage of rated play value, and according to a "menu" of available comps. Depending upon your betting level and how long you play these may include hotel rooms, meals, cash back, gift shop items, jackets, etc. or even air fare. A casino will do whatever they feel it takes to keep you coming back to them.

Comps and player databases are linked to enable better cost and profit control and to promote the Casino through direct mail to valuable players, on-the-spot rewards, special events and other sales efforts. A comp can be distributed during play, at the end of a session or when you leave.

The Players Club is usually found near Guest Service or at the VIP Service Desk at major casinos. Fill out a registration card and review the rules and rewards. Obtain a Players Club Card, (similar to a credit card), and join "special clubs" (i.e. For Seniors or High Rollers). Some Clubs are linked to other Players Clubs and sometimes have special tournaments for members only. Find out how to get your name in the player tracking computer and use your Players Card whenever you visit a casino. As rating points accumulate, you may be "promoted" to higher levels. Sometimes "on-the-spot" gifts are given in the play area.

Give your card to the dealer of a table game you want to join, (they will pass it to the Pit Boss or Floorperson). Present the card every time you move to a new table. A rating card will then be started. With automated player tracking systems your card will be "swiped" through a card reader and an entry made in your personal file.

Most slot machines are now equipped with card readers and have their own qualifying guidelines. When playing slot machines equipped to read Player Cards insert the card in the card receiver on the front of the slot machine. Watch the display window for your name and a greeting message to appear. Do not operate the slot machine until your card is read and recognized otherwise you will not receive credit for your play.

Visit casino's on Special Promotional Days, you may earn double or triple points for special events and on certain days of the week. Most casinos will offer some kind of special deal on the off days, Monday thru Thursday, just to fill seats.

Players who want to take every possible advantage when qualifying for comps have been known to do the following:

1.   Play only at casino's frequented by "locals" and those located away from "casino strips."

2.   The perception of action and a large bankroll is what counts. Buy-in with the largest amount of money possible, and buy-in and cash-out often. This is known in the business as "false dropping." You can walk into the casino with only $100 in your pocket but have a rating card that values you as a $1000 player.

3.   Make their first bet at least $25 (then lower bets when the Floorperson is not watching as intently).

4.   Take a periodic "time-out," by asking the dealer to hold their seat while they walk around for a few minutes (the play time clock is still running).

Learn to make friends with dealers and Floor people, and always be pleasant but firm in your request for comps. Remember the old saying, "you get more with honey than you do with vinegar". Whether you are a frequent visitor to the casinos or only there once or twice a year you should always join a Players Club and enjoy the benefits of Casino Comps. Don't miss out on your share. After all, you've earned it.

F.A.Q.'s.

Will I Always Win If I Count Cards?

No. Card counters do not win every time they play. What they have is a long-term advantage over the casino, which means that over the course of time they will win more money than they will lose. In the short term, such as a single playing session. they can lose.

Do The Casino's Cheat?

It would be extremely unusual for a casino to attempt any form of cheating. For a start, they don't need to. The odds of every game are weighed in favor of the house, in some games more than others, and although players will get their fair share of wins in the end the casino will always come out ahead.

Also, most of the casinos are now heavily regulated by overseeing impartial agencies known as gaming boards or gaming commissions which are, in most cases, staffed by state police. Individual casinos have to strictly abide by an inflexible set of rules and procedures known as "internal controls". Any deviation from these procedures can and frequently does result in the casino being disciplined and can often result in stiff fines being imposed. Something as severe as a casino purposely cheating could ultimately result in the loss of that casino's gaming license, in effect shutting them down. No casino is going to take the risk of that happening to them.

Does It Matter Where I Sit?

When playing basic strategy the odds that either you or the person sitting next to you will make a winning hand are exactly the same. It may seem at times that the person on a particular playing spot is overly lucky or that you couldn't get a winning hand if your life depended on it, and in the short term that may be so, but over time it all evens out. Whether you sit on the first, last or middle spot will make no difference to your win or loss over the long term.

For card counters, it can be helpful to sit near the end, ("third base"), since you will be able to observe more cards before you make a decision upon your play. But this will only apply if you are making the correct deviations from basic strategy.

Does The House Have The Edge Because I Go First?

The main bulk of the house advantage comes from the fact that you have to go first. If you get 19 and the dealer gets 19 it is a push, you get 20 and the dealer gets 20 it is also a push but, if you go bust and then the dealer goes bust..... You Lose. The house's edge based on this effect alone is very high, over 7.5 percent.

This is why Basic Strategy play is so important, prompting you to stand on a small total and not risk going over when the dealer shows a small card and has a greater chance of busting.

Should I Insure A Good Hand, (19, 20), Against The Dealer's Ace?

The phrase "Insurance" is a little deceptive. You are not really protecting your hand by taking Insurance because it is actually considered to be a separate bet against the house, gambling on whether or not the dealer does or does not have a ten as the hole card. It's as simple as that.

The mathematics of this wager is that out of the thirteen possible cards that the dealer might have, (Ace thru King), only four of them are 10's making the true odds of this bet 4 out of 13 or 3.25 to 1. A big difference from the paltry offer of 2 to 1 that the casino is offering you.

Also you have to consider the fact that if you take the Insurance bet for the full amount, (half of your original bet), then you are really decreasing the amount of your potential win by half. The house comes out ahead either way.

The only time that you would consider taking the Insurance bet is if you are utilizing a count system and have reached a True Count of +3 or more - regardless of your hand total.

Does The Play Of Others Affect Me?

Have you ever been playing at a Blackjack table when one of the players who has been getting a run of bad luck has made the declaration, "I'm going to sit out a hand to change the cards" or has refused to take a double down or a split because "the dealer is lucky". Unfortunately I hear some variation of these comments every day. I have seen players who will drop their bets simply because the dealer has changed or as a result of seeing another player making, what is to them, a bad decision. I can tell you this from experience - it doesn't make a difference. The fact is, the way other people play their hands does not in any way determine whether or not you will win or lose, neither will it influence the dealer's hand.

The cards come out of the shoe in a completely random order, the sequence of which nobody could know. The fact that another player before you either does or does not take a card will not affect the odds of you either pulling a 5 on a 16 or getting an 8 to go with your 12. If the card is there then the card is there. Who's to say that he is not helping by removing a 10 before your much needed 5? The foolish or irrational plays by other players do not in any way affect your long term results. The flow of the cards may be altered, but the final results offset. You are just as likely to win a hand or lose a hand as the result of a player's "mistake" in play.

Does It Make A Difference When The Dealer Changes?

How many times have you seen a player drop his bet because the dealer changed, only to receive a twenty or a Blackjack on the next hand? Yes the new dealer did burn a card and yes, this does change the sequence of the coming shoe, but for better or worse, who knows? The same applies to the player who refuses to double his 11 proclaiming "I can't win a hand against this dealer" and then is promptly dealt the 10 he needed.

Playing proper basic strategy gives you the best odds of winning against the house with any given hand and by not following those guidelines you are just playing into the hands of the casino.

Is Blackjack The Same In Every Casino?

The playing rules are often different from one casino to the next and sometimes even within the same casino. Some tables may use single decks while others can use 2, 4, 6 or even 8 decks of cards. In some casinos the dealer's must stand on soft 17 and in others they will hit. Some will allow the players to surrender or double down after splitting pairs and others will not. There are other rules, some which favor the casino more than the player and others vice versa. The amount of times you may be allowed to split a hand, especially Aces, can differ. A long time ago someone once said to me that "all casinos are the same and the only thing that changes is the carpet". Not so. The number of decks of cards being used and the rules being played determines how much an edge that particular casino has. Hitting the soft 17 alone can add a full 1% to the house advantage.

If you unsure of the differentiating rules of the casino you are attending then ask the dealer before you play. Follow the old adage and "look before you leap", it could mean the difference between a successful or losing night.

I Lost Five Hands In A Row So I Should Win The Next, Right?

Wrong. The cards don't care that you lost five hands in a row, neither do they care if you win five in a row. The chances of you winning or losing the next hand is completely independent upon whether or not you won, lost or tied the previous three, five or even ten hands. Never make your next bet based on the assumption that you are due to win, you are only likely to be disappointed.

Cheats And Scams.
The Darker Side Of Blackjack.

Warning: The subject matter discussed in this chapter is printed here solely for educational purposes. Any real-time use of this information in a casino can be considered <u>ILLEGAL</u> and could result in arrest and prosecution.

Ever since the game of Blackjack was devised there have been those who have tried to beat it, by whatever means necessary. The very first day that Blackjack was played there was probably somebody trying to cheat. Many of these methods are so crude and obvious that they are normally caught almost immediately but there are also some that are cunning, resourceful and even daring that if used skillfully could take some considerable time to become detected.... if at all.

Some of these techniques are as follows:

Past Posting.

Probably the most common form of player cheating and the easiest to attempt is a method called "past posting." This is the simple act of either adding to, taking away from or in any way changing your bet after the hand has been dealt.

A player, normally sitting at the first or last position at the table, with a keen eye on the dealer and a quick hand would attempt this strategy which requires nerves of steel and a quick, concise maneuver.

The dealers and Pit Bosses are well aware of this technique and are watching for it. The first time you get caught, you might escape by claiming ignorance or acting drunk. You didn't realize it was to late or you thought it was the next hand etc. After that they will be watching you closely. Try it again and you're asking for a security escort to a back room!

The Double Double.

Similar in design to past posting the "double double" is a way of increasing the size of the bet when it is most to your advantage but, in some ways, is actually easier to get away with.

The player, usually sitting at the last gaming position, (third base), is betting his normal wager, for instance $25. When he acquires a good double hand, such as 11 against a 6 or 10 against a 5, he waits until the dealer is paying the least attention to him and, acting as if he doesn't know any better, places his double bet on top of his original wager.

In most cases the dealer will see this but will probably assume they are dealing to "just another dumb beginner who doesn't know any better", taking it down and placing it in it's correct place and continuing the hand. No harm - no foul. Nothing is suspected but..... if the dealer does not spot this simple but effective trick, either is not paying attention or is distracted, they will get to the hand and, as most dealers do, pause and allow the player to double his bet, now $50, in effect doubling the double.

Depending upon the competence of the dealer this technique could be applied several times before suspicion is aroused.

Marked Cards.

On the shoe games marked card scams usually start with a loophole in the casino's card control procedures. Inadequate card control is not a problem limited to a few small casinos but is a constant problem with casino's and card rooms worldwide.

For example, New Jersey is considered to have exceptionally tight card control which continues even after the cards are used. All decks are sealed in bags and picked up by the Division of Gaming Enforcement, but still marked cards have, over the course of time, surfaced in every single New Jersey Casino. In the past marked cards have also been discovered in major Las Vegas casinos and in Reno. A closer look at the card controls suggests that the scams may have been going on for some time. Virtually every card room and casino in the world has had to deal with this type of scam at one time or another.

Sometimes it might be that the cards were professionally marked, probably with a laser, sometimes it might be a more common type of work known as "two-way line shade." These scams are amongst the most difficult to detect. "Shade" can be made with, primarily, pure grain alcohol and a minute amount of the most permanent, fade-proof ink or dye available, preferably aniline. Shade is almost colorless but provides enough of a tint to slightly shade the card and is most commonly used to gray the white areas of the card. Shade can be applied by hand, (brush), or mechanically with the help of an airbrush and templates to accurately position the marks.

If a "line" of circles, diamonds, squares or any part of the back design of the card is shaded then the eye will see those marks as a darker line. Cheaters tend to prefer the shoe game when playing shade because the top card is a consistent, stationary target, (unlike pitch games), and the action of dealing the top card creates a contrast with the next card to be dealt.

Once the cards are marked they now somehow have to get to the game. This can be accomplished in many ways but most would include the collusion of an employee. A Pit Boss, Security Guard or even a

Janitor. In rare cases cards have been stolen during the delivery process and even from the manufacturer. If the cards have to be resealed then this is no problem. An experienced crook can get in and out of a factory wrapped card case in just minutes, without ever breaking the seal. Some controls may even allow the decks to be opened prior to transporting them to the game.

There are numerous tests a casino can make to detect a marked deck. Black lights, certain filters, angled light, and the "riffle" test, to name a few, can all be employed. There are even tests that might help detect the marks during play such as looking to the right or left of the shoe, throwing your eyes out of focus, and reading from a distance, all designed to stop the eye from focusing much as you would with one of those aggravating "magic eye" pictures. (I find them aggravating because I can't do them. I guess we all have our faults).

On the pitch games, where the players are allowed to touch the cards, much simpler methods of marking the cards can be employed. One of these methods would be to "daub" the cards. Daub is a sticky substance, which is used to physically mark the cards. This could be anything from lipstick or make-up, to paint or even shoe polish. A player holding their cards would discreetly apply daub to a finger which would then mark a card in a predetermined position with a faint, almost unnoticeable, smudge. There have been cases where players, usually men, have hidden small pots of daub either behind their tie or under a wristwatch but it is probably easier for women to apply daub by subtly touching a finger to their lip or face, maybe feigning an itch, before picking up their cards.

The simplest method of all to mark cards is known as "thumbnailing". This is exactly what it sounds like. A player, while holding their cards, will discreetly squeeze their fingers embedding the imprint of their thumbnail into the corner of the card marking or indenting a specific location. While this may seem to be a fairly obvious maneuver an unsuspecting dealer may not notice this for many hands.

The Shoe Switch.

This is an operation I have never actually witnessed first hand but have had the opportunity to see on a copy of a surveillance tape.

The dealer shuffled the cards as normal, then offered the cards to a player for the cut. This is when the scam took place. The player, who was in collusion with the dealer, had placed a bag under the table. He waited fro the dealer to shuffle, then reached under the table into his bag and pulled out an entire shoe of pre-arranged cards. Six decks worth!

As the dealer offered the cards to him the player, in one fluid movement, grabbed them with one hand and pulled them under the table into his bag while placing the other set of cards in front of the dealer, which the dealer then placed smoothly into the shoe as if nothing was amiss and commenced dealing. None of the other players at the table said a word.

A few minutes later a shadow fell across the table. The camera panned back to show the table, and all of its customers, surrounded by a large contingent of security officers.

As you have probably noticed, many casino's have their shoes attached to the tables with a cord or chain and, at the end of each shoe, the dealer's are trained to loudly announce "shuffle", sometimes even having to wait for a Supervisor's approval. Now you know why.

Cheating Dealers.

While the house will not usually go out of its way to cheat you, (they don't have to), it is possible from time to time to run across the occasional unscrupulous dealer. The honesty of the dealer can be critical to winning. It doesn't matter how powerful your strategy is, or how much of a mathematical genius you may be, it will be extremely difficult for you to win against a cheating dealer.

The most common way of cheating is by the use of sleight of hand. Sleight of hand means the use of manual dexterity to manipulate cards and deal cards from other than the top of the deck. The most widespread type of sleight in Blackjack is the dealing of "seconds". This means dealing the second card from the top of the deck while leaving the top card in place. What the dealer is doing, (while he is adjusting his chips or paying players off, or while he's looking underneath his up card when it is a ten or an Ace checking to see if he has a ten or an Ace underneath), is moving the deck around at different angles, and it is on these occasions that he has a chance to crimp the top card and take a peek at it. Now, once he knows what the top card is he'll know whether or not he needs to deal seconds in order to save himself the top card so that he can make his hand.

The way dealers are trained to pick up cards in a casino is from left to right or from right to left all in one sweep, keeping the cards for each player's hand together so that the hand may be reconstructed at a later time should the player dispute the dealer's call as to whether he won or lost the hand. It is rare that you'll see a dealer picking up the cards in any way other than in a smooth order from his left to right or from right to left, however it has been known for a dealer to pick up the cards and arrange them in a high-low stack, "stacking" the cards.

Another way for the dealer to cheat is the "false shuffle". Also known as the "pull-through" shuffle, this technique utilizes a unique false riffle shuffle that, although it looks like the deck is being shuffled correctly, will keep the entire deck intact. The false shuffle can be used effectively not only in Blackjack but in any card game and, performed correctly, can be almost undetectable.

The false riffle shuffle, with practice, can be done very rapidly and gives the appearance not only of thoroughly shuffling but also of capping each shuffle with a solid cut. The key to executing this maneuver lies in lightly and loosely riffling the cards and then gently pushing the halves inward. After the side-squaring motion and without groping or fumbling, the original top block of cards is pulled out intact with the left hand. Everyone at the table can clearly see that the dealer has thoroughly "shuffled" the deck when his fingers grasp the sides of the deck and push the interlaced card together. Only after that "push-through" does the dealer then shield the deck to falsely square its ends. This permits the dealer to then pull the deck apart again - with all the cards in their original positions.

The "Faro Shuffle", also known as the "Weave Shuffle" is a technique that perfectly interlaces the cards. It is not a false shuffle, but properly speaking a controlled shuffle. An "Out" faro is one which retains the top and bottom cards after the shuffle and an "In" faro keeps changing the top and bottom cards.

If eight perfect out faro's are performed in a row, the deck will return to the original order it was in before the shuffle took place giving it the appearance of a properly executed riffle shuffle.

Team Play.

While it is not necessarily classified as cheating, there have emerged a number of professional card counting teams that will travel around the country, from casino to casino, usually winning large sums of money wherever they go. These teams consist of groups of men and women who will work together as a unit, usually taking over an entire Blackjack table, in order to gain the maximum possible advantage against the casino.

This particular method of play can be tremendously effective. As one team member is utilizing a simple plus-minus count, another will be tracking Aces and tens, while yet another will be using a more advanced count system. One more member will be either segment or shuffle tracking. During the game they will discreetly signal to each other their findings either by the placements of their bets within the betting circle or by other pre-arranged signals. The girls, normally standing behind the players, handle the money management removing chips or dispensing cash in predetermined amounts to the players at the table.

Used individually each of these systems has the ability to significantly alter the house advantage and bring them ahead of the casino. When all of these techniques are combined then the effects can be enormous and, to an unsuspecting casino, devastating.

At the foremost of these teams are the "Highland Group", run by Tommy Highland and Bill Cuff, and the "M.I.T. Group", which stems from the prestigious M.I.T. University in Cambridge, Massachusetts. Both of these teams, staffed by very intelligent, highly motivated and exceptionally well trained individuals, have proven themselves again and again to be especially dangerous to the house and, as you can imagine, have found themselves barred from casinos across the country.

Surveillance.

Although the casinos have always had the home court advantage, that hasn't stopped the crooks from attempting to cheat the house. In the old days panels of one-way mirrors were installed in the ceilings over the casino floor. Surveillance people would walk back and forth balancing on narrow catwalks while watching the casino floor. With binoculars in hand, they would monitor both the players and the dealers for any signs of cheating. They maneuvered through spider webs and around posts and rafters in the dark.

Today's modern casinos are completely different. Outfitted with hundreds of cameras that can rotate, pivot and zoom in on a pinhead, able to read your wristwatch from the other side of the room. These cameras are housed in those half-spherical bubbles that you see mounted from the ceilings. They send video signals that are fed into dozens of monitors with videotapes rolling. While it is not possible for all of the cameras' signals can be shown on a monitor at all times, the video can be later reviewed. The surveillance crew must switch back and forth between cameras, focusing more on the busy-betting areas and the cashiers' cages. If the pit is suspicious of a cheat or if a high roller steps into the game, the Pit Boss will call up to surveillance to make sure they are watching the action at that table, or so you think.

Actually nowadays, in most casino's, the whole system is computerized. A network of several hundred tiny digital cameras are mounted throughout the casino areas. These areas include not only the casino floor, but also the hotel areas, restaurants, bars, parking lots, stairwells and elevators. It is quite safe to assume that the second you set foot onto casino property you are on film.

As these cameras sense movement, they begin processing a digital signal to a computer. Surveillance software interprets any actions it senses and the most questionable of those will appear on one of several main monitors where the surveillance crew will be stationed. Because the footage is digital and fully indexed it can be immediately accessed and cross-referenced with other footage taken, even if it happened as much as six months earlier. There are no archived tapes to search through and no hours and hours of rewinding and playing of videotapes. Everything is stored in one central database and immediately accessible. Nowadays nothing is hidden from "the eye in the sky".

Electronic Equipment And Devices.

Warning: As I expressed earlier, the use or attempted use of this type of equipment in a casino is <u>ILLEGAL</u> and, in order to set an example and to protect their assets, the casino <u>WILL</u> prosecute. The information discussed in this chapter is printed here solely for educational purposes and should be treated as such.

With today's advances in computer technology it goes without saying that sooner or later there are going to be some enterprising individuals who have conceived various "devices" and means with which to try and beat the casino. While I do not condone the use of this type of equipment, (I think it can only lead to trouble), I don't think that any up to date book on the study of Blackjack would be complete without at least a little information upon the subject.

Glims.

A glim, also known as a glimmer, twinkle or shiner, can be any reflective surface strategically placed in order to obtain a glimpse of the dealer's hole card. All a cheat needs is the slightest glance in order to give himself a huge advantage. Such items could consist of simple objects such as a small thin cigarette case, a wristwatch laid on the table or even a polished coin. One of the most devious methods I have heard of consisted of a prism built into a plastic ice cube. Sitting in just the right position a player can merely look down into his half finished drink in order to catch a reflection of the card as it is being dealt.

Rumor has it that one of these suspected cheats was caught only because of the temper tantrum he threw when a cocktail server started to walk away with his finished drink.

Card Counting Perfect Strategy Computers.

Heralded as the ultimate card counting weapon a Blackjack computer is capable of performing millions of calculations prior to rendering a decision. It bases all of its decisions on the exact composition of the remaining cards, (perfect Blackjack), which totally makes obsolete the playing of mental Blackjack.

Using one of these concealed high-speed computers, (also known as "toe-tappers"), it can be possible to achieve extraordinary profits while playing Blackjack. A concealed, miniaturized, self-contained computer worn under the clothing outputs signals that only the player can feel. These signals reveal to the player everything he needs to know in order to win consistently at the game. It is a proven, scientific way to completely eliminate the casino's advantage.

These computers are considered to be so good that it takes Blackjack to the point where almost no skill is required from the player and they can be so easy to learn that the player does not even need to know how to count cards or even Basic Strategy.

Another major advantage of a computer is the longevity factor. Simply stated, you can play for hours on end without any fatigue and there won't be the usual "heat" that a card counter may often endure, since you can play with only half of the normal bet spread a counter must use and still maintain a higher advantage.

Simply put, the computer is able to do everything for you including telling you how to play each individual hand, when to increase and decrease your bets and when to add and remove hands.

It also takes into consideration other players and also allows for each particular casino's rule variations, dealer hits soft 17, how many times you can split, etc.

Best of all, it totally eliminates chance and turns the game into a science. In fact, as a result of using a computer you can expect to win an incredible nine out of ten sessions whereas an expert card counter could expect to only win six or seven out of ten sessions.

The computers of today are now so small and can easily be disguised as an everyday object such as a walkman or a hearing aid or can be cunningly concealed inside of a cigarette case holder or, (with today's technology in computer chips), a wristwatch, beeper or cell phone. This is the prime reason why casinos will not allow the use of any kind of electronic device either at or near the tables.

Pictured here are two computers, a pair of shoes, and a hand keyboard used by the player for home practice. Notice the taper in the middle of the shoes. This is how the player receives the outputs from the computer. The input switches are concealed in the toe area of the shoe and cannot be seen in this picture.

In the middle of the picture you get a better look at the output tapers that are normally located in the middle of the shoe.

The following is a portion of an article that appeared in The Press of Atlantic City on July 4th, 1987 by staff writer Daniel Heneghan.

(Reprinted by permission of The Press of Atlantic City.)

ATLANTIC CITY - Gamblers who walk softly but wear big boots may be costing casinos millions of dollars because the boots conceal tiny computers that give them an edge at the game of blackjack.

"It is a very serious problem at this point, and one that is growing by the day," said Paul Burst, executive vice president of Del Webb's Claridge Casino Hotel. In fact, officials at one casino estimated that the concealed computers could be costing the casinos as much as $20 million a year in lost revenue.

Leon Drew, an assistant shift manager at Harrah's Marine Hotel Casino said some of the players have tempered their greed in order to avoid drawing attention to themselves.

"There's no way to tell how many people are taking out moderate amounts," he said. But both Burst and Drew said the computers are so accurate that they successfully tell gamblers to make what otherwise would appear to be irrational decisions.

The computer is about the size of a cigarette pack and as a player inputs information about all the cards as they are being dealt, the computer can determine with astonishing accuracy what the next card is and can tell the player to bet accordingly, the casino official said.

Officials explained that players can conceal four tiny switches in their shoes and use them to input the value of each card into the computer by moving their big toes up or down. The computer then sends signals to the player by way of buzzing or vibrating electrodes taped to the player's body. All of the wiring is concealed under the clothing, and the computer itself is generally strapped to the player's leg and hidden by the boot.

Brenda Smith, an assistant casino manager, said that the computers first appeared in casinos more than a year ago. She added that Atlantic City casinos are easier targets than gaming halls elsewhere for players with computers. She said the crowded conditions can make it much harder for such individuals to be detected.

There are other types of devices that enable one person watching the game to input the information and have the signals sent by radio waves to a partner who can appear to be paying no attention to the game. In addition, the computer can be programmed to play by Atlantic City rules or the rules used in other jurisdictions and can take into account the number of decks used in the game.

"We've received only a handful of incident reports at the casinos about these," said Anthony

Parrillo, director of the gaming division. But he noted that it isn't the kind of information that the casinos are required to report to state regulators.

Drew said the computers are so good that they completely eliminate the house's advantage in blackjack and give the player a five to seven percent edge over the house.

The Press Of Atlantic City, New Jersey.

Important Note:

In 1985, the Governor of Nevada signed into law, Senate Bill 467. The pertinent statute in Nevada states:

"It is unlawful for any person at a licensed gaming establishment to use, or possess with the intent to use, any device to assist in projecting the outcome of the game."

The statute goes on to say that a first-time offender may be imprisoned for a period of 1 to 10 years, or be fined up to $10,000, or both. A second offense is mandatory imprisonment. In other words, if you're caught with a computer or similar device in the casino, even if you did not yet use it, you may be hit with stiff fines or even jail time!

This is too big a gamble in my book! New Jersey has a similar statute regarding the use of electronic, electrical and mechanical devices:

"Except as specifically permitted by the commission, no person shall possess with the intent to use, or actually use, at any table game, either by himself or in concert with others, any calculator, computer, or other electronic, electrical or mechanical device to assist in projecting an outcome at any table game or in keeping track of or analyzing the cards having been dealt, the changing probabilities of any table game, or the playing strategies to be utilized".

All states with legalized gambling have employed some version of these laws, all with equally severe consequences for offenders.

Conclusion.

Now that you have completed reading this book you probably know more about the game of Blackjack than 90% of the people in the casino, including those who work behind the tables. You must still remember that even though it is possible to turn the odds to your favor it is not a guaranteed win. One night I was playing Blackjack at a casino where the dealer was only cutting off about one half to a third of a deck on a six deck shoe. Towards the end of the shoe you could imagine my astonishment and delight when the count reached +20. With only one deck remaining in the shoe this was a true count. I was ecstatic. I put up my maximum bet and received a 20, the dealer pulled a Blackjack, and I lost. Now the count had reached an incredible true +22, a card counter's dream. Out went my maximum bet once more. Everybody at the table made 20's and

Blackjacks except, guess who, me. It seemed it must have been the only 5 left in the deck and it somehow was able to find my hand. I now had 15 against the dealer's 10 and with a plus count this high I can't hit. I have to hope he has a small card and busts but as you can guess that wasn't how it happened. The dealer made 20 and I walked away losing. This just goes to show that even with a shoe this much to your advantage, over 80% of the cards being tens or Aces, it is still very possible to lose the hand and, even though it is possible at times to turn the odds to your favor, the element of luck still exists. Nothing is guaranteed!

This is the reason why money management is so important. Remember, never exceed your maximum bet and always stay within your bankroll.

GOOD LUCK.

Glossary.

ace	The best card in the deck. Totals as 1 or 11.
bank	House money, the chips in the tray used for paying wins.
bankroll	Your money. The amount you are able to play with.
basic strategy	The correct way to play any possible hand in the game of Blackjack.
bet	Wager. The amount you are willing to play each hand.
bet spread	The difference between your lowest and highest bet.
blackjack	Natural 21. 21 with 2 cards.
blooper	Mistake, error, blunder.
bust	To go over. Your hand total exceeds 21.
cage	The casino booth where you change your chips for cash.
card counter	Person who has the ability to keep track of the cards.

card counting	Method of keeping track of which cards have been played, and which have not.
cashing out	Changing your gaming tokens for cash.
casino	The facility where gambling and games of chance are played.
cheating	Deceiving or manipulating the casino into paying you when you should not be paid.
chips	Cheques, tokens used as money within the casino.
clumping	Method of following groups of cards through the shuffle.
complimentaries	Comps. Rewards or gifts given to valued customers based upon rated play.
counting cards	Technique of keeping track of which cards have been played, and which have not during the course of play.
cover play	Subtle mistakes used to convince the casino that you are not counting cards.
crimp	To slightly bend a card or a portion of a card in order to covertly see its identity.

156

cut card	The colored plastic card used by the dealer to cut the cards. Also notifies the dealer of the impending end of the shoe.
daub	A sticky substance used to mark the cards.
dealer	The person you are playing against. The person paying or taking your money.
decision	The choice you make affecting the outcome of the hand.
deck	A group of 52 cards.
devices	Equipment or machinery designed to cheat the casino.
double-down	Adding to your bet on the first 2 cards because you are confident you will win. You will receive 1 card only.
edge	The advantage given to either you or the casino at any given time.
etiquette	Protocol. Do's and don'ts of the game.
even money	Being paid the same amount as wagered.
eviction	Expelled from the casino, asked to leave.

eye in the sky	Surveillance. The cameras in the ceilings watching you at all times.
face card	Picture Card. 10, Jack, Queen or King. (Any suit).
face-down	Card is on the layout with the reverse uppermost, hiding the identity of the card.
face-up	Card is on the layout with the front uppermost, showing the identity of the card.
false drop	Cashing out chips and re-buying in to make it look like you are playing with more money than you actually have.
false shuffle	Method of making it look like the cards have been correctly shuffled when they have not.
floorperson	The person in the Pit responsible for a number of Blackjack games. Answerable to the Pit Boss.
gambling	The act of playing games of chance for money.
glim	Glimmer. A small reflective device used to cheat by seeing the identity of the cards as they are dealt.

grind	Slang term for the house edge. Grinding away at the players bankrolls.
hand	The cards dealt to each playing position.
hard total	A hand total containing no Aces or where Ace is counted as one only, otherwise you would bust.
hit	Take a card.
hole card	The dealer's down card.
house	Casino.
house advantage	The percentage or small edge the casino has over you at any given time.
house rules	The rules of the game each casino must abide by. (May differ slightly from casino to casino).
hunch	Guess. A decision based on instinct or intuition.
insurance	A separate bet offered by the house when the dealer shows an Ace.
layout	The cloth playing surface.
marked cards	Any cards that have been marked, altered or tampered with.
minus count	When the running or true count falls below 0.

money management   Methods of controlling your bankroll in order to gain maximum advantage.

odds   Payout amounts. Even money, 3 - 2, etc

past posting   Adding to or taking away from a bet once the hand has been dealt.

percentage   The amount of edge the casino has on the player at any given time.

pit   The area behind the tables. (Employees only).

Pit Boss   The person in charge of the entire pit area.

pitch   Blackjack game dealt from the dealer's hand instead of a shoe.

player   Person playing the game.

plus count   When the running or true count is 1 or above.

push   Stand off, tie. The hand neither wins nor loses.

rack   The container holding the table bank.

rated play   The casino's way of tracking players for which they give complimentaries.

running count	The total of high cards versus low cards that have been played.
scam	To cheat. Any method or technique used to illegally defeat the casino.
seconds	A method of dealer cheating where they will deal the second card of the deck rather than the card from the top.
shade	Marking cards by lightly tinting certain areas.
shoe	The box device the cards are dealt from in order to ensure fair play.
shuffle	The randomizing of the cards by the dealer.
shuffle tracking	Method of tracking or following the location of certain cards through the shuffle.
slug	Group of cards.
soft total	A hand total containing an Ace where the Ace is counted as 11.
split	A hand containing a pair which is split into 2 or more separate hands.
stacking	Stacking the deck. Setting the cards in a predetermined order.
stand	Electing to stay with the total you have.

161

sucker bet	Any bet considered to be hugely advantageous to the house.
surrender	Giving up half of your bet in order to back out of an unfavorable hand.
surveillance	The "eye in the sky". Casino department tasked with the responsibility of monitoring all casino areas.
table limits	The minimum or maximum bet the casino will allow you to bet at a table. (Can differ from table to table).
team play	A group of individuals playing together as a unit in order to achieve the maximum advantage possible over the casino.
technique	Method or procedure used specifically in play.
thumbnailing	Using the finger or thumbnail to mark or indent a corner of a card.
toke	Tip or gratuity given to the dealer for good service.
true count	The total of high cards versus low cards that have been played divided by the amount of decks remaining in the shoe.

unit	Set portions of your bankroll in which you make your bets.
variation play	Altered strategies of play based upon the true count.
wager	Bet. The amount you are willing to gamble on a hand.

With over 15 years of experience in the casino industry working behind the tables at casinos in England, aboard various Cruise lines and throughout the United States, Stephen Mead is a true expert upon the inner workings of the casino.

Also the author of "You Can Win!" Mead has written and published articles for several gaming publications. Beginner To Pro is his second book.

VARIATION CHART --- HI-LO

X	2	3	4	5	6	7	8	9	10	A
12	+3 S	+2 S	-1 H	-2 H	-1 H					
13	-1 H	-2 H	-4 H	-5 H	-5 H					
14			-7 H	-8 H	-8 H					
15	-6 H	-7 H	-8 H	-10 H	-10 H	+10 S	+8 S	+4 S	+10 S	
16	-9 H	-11 H	-12 H	-13 H	-14 H	-8 S	+7 S	+5 S	+1 S	+8 S
17										
2-2			-4 H	-10 H	-13 H	-28 H	-5 H			
3-3	-1 H	-5 H	-8 H	-10 H	-14 H	-29 H	+4 Sp			
4-4			+15Sp	+6Sp	+1 Sp					
6-6	-2 H	-5 H	-7 H	-9 H	-11 H					
7-7	-10 H	-12 H	-14 H	-15 H	-21 H	-28 H	+5 Sp			
8-8										+8 S
9-9	-3 S	-4 S	-6 S	-7 S	-7 S	+3 Sp	-9 S	-10 S		+3 Sp
10-10,11		+8 Sp	+6 Sp	+5 Sp	+4 Sp					
A-A	-12 H	-13 H	-13 H	-14 H	-15 H	-10 H	-9 H	-8 H	-9 H	-4 H
7	+23 D	+16 D	+12 D	+9 D	+9 D	+14 D	+7 D			
8	+13 D	+9 D	+5 D	+3 D	+1 D	+14 D	+7 D			
9	+1 D	-1	-3 H	-5 H	-7 H	+3 D	-7 D			
10	-9 H	-10 H	-11 H	-12 H	-14 H	-7 H	-5 H	-2 H	+4 D	+4 D
11	-12 H	-13 H	-13 H	-14 H	-15 H	-10 H	-7 H	-5 H	-5 H	+1 D
A-2	-13 D	+14 D	+3 D	-1 H	-2 H					
A-3	-14 D	+7 D	+1 D	-2 H	-5 H					
A-4	+18 D	+7 D	-1 H	-5 H	-10 H					
A-5	+15 D	+4 D	-3 H	-7 H	-13 H					
A-6	+1 D	-4 H	-8 H	-11 H	-14 H					
A-7	+1 D	-3 S	-7 S	-9 S	-11 S					
A-8	+8 D	+5 D	+3 D	+1 D	+4 D					
A-9	+10 D	+8 D	+6 D	+5 D	+4 D					

TAKE INSURANCE ON +3

BASIC STRATEGY

X	2	3	4	5	6	7	8	9	10	A
9	H	D	D	D	D	H	H	H	H	H
10	D	D	D	D	D	D	D	D	H	H
11	D	D	D	D	D	D	D	D	D	H
12	H	H	H	S	S	H	H	H	H	H
13	S	S	S	S	S	H	H	H	H	H
14	S	S	S	S	S	H	H	H	H	H
15	S	S	S	S	S	H	H	H	H	H
16	S	S	S	S	S	H	H	H	H	H
2-2	Sp	Sp	Sp	Sp	Sp	Sp	H	H	H	H
3-3	Sp	Sp	Sp	Sp	Sp	Sp	H	H	H	H
4-4	H	H	H	Sp	Sp	H	H	H	H	H
6-6	Sp	Sp	Sp	Sp	Sp	H	H	H	H	H
7-7	Sp	Sp	Sp	Sp	Sp	Sp	H	H	H	H
8-8	Sp	Sp	Sp	Sp	Sp	Sp	Sp	Sp	Sp	Sp
9-9	Sp	Sp	Sp	Sp	Sp	S	Sp	Sp	S	S
A-A	Sp	Sp	Sp	Sp	Sp	Sp	Sp	Sp	Sp	Sp
A-2	H	H	H	D	D	H	H	H	H	H
A-3	H	H	D	D	D	H	H	H	H	H
A-4	H	H	D	D	D	H	H	H	H	H
A-5	H	H	D	D	D	H	H	H	H	H
A-6	H	D	D	D	D	H	H	H	H	H
A-7	S	D	D	D	D	S	S	H	H	H

H = HIT S = STAND D = DOUBLE DOWN Sp = SPLIT

167